LET'S VISIT THAILAND

Let's visit
THAILAND

FRANCES WILKINS

First published 1985
© Frances Wilkins 1985

ACKNOWLEDGEMENTS

The Author and Publishers are grateful to the following organizations and individuals for permission to reproduce copyright photographs in this book:
    Colorpix, Imag, International Photobank, Eugénie Peter and Photothéque Vautier-de Nanxe.

CIP data
Wilkins, Frances
    Let's visit Thailand
    1. Thailand – Social life and customs – Juvenile literature
    I. Title
    959.3'044   DS568
ISBN 0 222 00982 9

Burke Publishing Company Limited
Pegasus House, 116-120 Golden Lane, London EC1Y 0TL, England.
Burke Publishing (Canada) Limited
Registered Office: 20 Queen Street West, Suite 3000, Box 30, Toronto, Canada M5H 1V5.
Burke Publishing Company Inc.
Registered Office: 333 State Street, PO Box 1740, Bridgeport, Connecticut 06601, U.S.A.
Filmset in Baskerville by Graphiti (Hull) Ltd., Hull, England.
Printed in Singapore by Tien Wah Press (Pte.) Ltd.

Contents

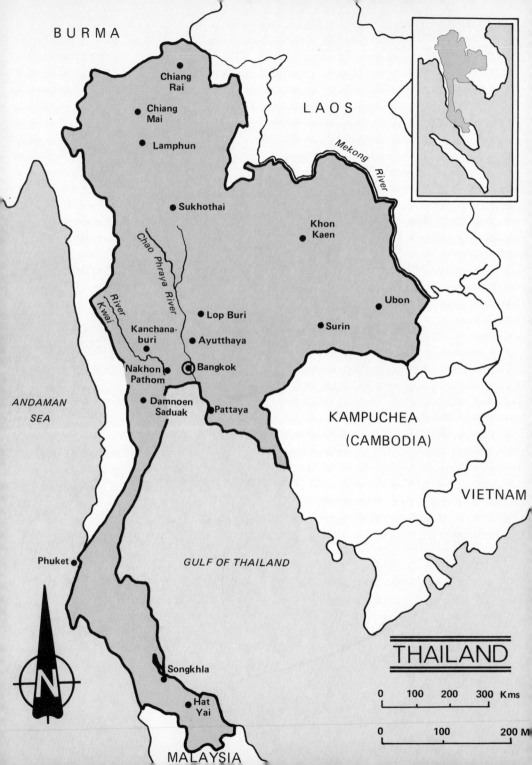

The Land and the People

Thailand has been called the "Land of Smiles", and on the whole the Thais have good reason to be happy. With large agricultural and mineral resources, Thailand is far more prosperous than many nations in the Far East. The country is situated in the centre of South-east Asia and covers over 513,000 square kilometres (about 198,000 square miles). Although Thailand is more than twice the size of the British Isles, and just a little smaller than France, it has a population of only fifty million. It is not, therefore, densely populated but the number of inhabitants is growing at a rate of two per cent a year.

Thailand is shaped rather like an axe with the handle pointing south. It is bordered by Burma on the north and west, by Laos on the north and north-east, by Kampuchea on the east and by Malaysia on the south. The Mekong River forms part of the border between Laos and Thailand.

The central area of Thailand consists of a low, flat plain. This plain is criss-crossed by innumerable rivers and canals, and is the most fertile area of the country. The north-eastern region forms a high arid plateau, while the north and the extreme south are both mountainous. The highest peak is about 2,600 metres (8,500 feet).

Thailand's climate is tropical and very humid. There are three

7

The "Golden Triangle", where Thailand, Burma and Laos meet

seasons: hot (March to May), rainy (June to October) and cool (November to February). In the hot season the average temperature is about 32° Centigrade (90° Fahrenheit). It often reaches 37° Centigrade (102° Fahrenheit) in April, and even in the so-called "cool" season the average temperature is still about 25° Centigrade (75° Fahrenheit).

The people of Thailand, the Thais, originally came from the Yangtze Valley of China. They are said to have founded an empire there as early as A.D. 650. Over the centuries they were increasingly persecuted by the Chinese, and by about the thirteenth century A.D. they had nearly all moved south into what is now called Thailand.

Although most of the people now living in Thailand are Thais, there are also about one million Malaysians, living mainly in the south of the country near the Malaysian border.

8

Thailand was known as Siam until just before the Second World War. Then the Thais decided to call their country "Thailand", which can be translated as "Land of the Free". This country is the only one in South-east Asia which has never been a colony or dominion of any other country.

Thailand is a constitutional monarchy. This means that the King is the Head of State, but that a National Assembly assists the King in his ruling of the country. The National Assembly in Thailand is divided into two houses—the Senate and the House of Representatives. The 225 members of the Senate are appointed by the King for a term of six years, and they must not be under 35 years of age or members of any political party. The 301 members of the House of Representatives are elected by the Thai people and serve for four years. The members must be aged at least 25. If a vacancy occurs, through death or retirement, a new member can be elected but only for the rest of the four-year term. All Thais aged twenty and over have the right to vote in elections.

The capital of Thailand is generally known as Bangkok. This name comes from *Bang Kok* meaning "the village of olives". Its official name, however, is Krung Thep Mana Nakhon, which is abbreviated in the Thai language to Kaw Thaw Maw. It is a sprawling metropolis of six million people—by far the largest city in Thailand. Most of Bangkok stands on the east bank of the Chao Phraya River but its industrial area is largely situated on the west bank, in the Thonburi district. Bangkok is also Thailand's most important port, in spite of the fact that it is

Flooding is common during the rainy season. This photograph shows a flooded street in Bangkok, Thailand's capital city

situated 35 kilometres (22 miles) up river from the sea.

The second largest city in Thailand is Chiang Mai, with about one million inhabitants. Its name means "the new city", although it was founded several hundred years ago in the mid-thirteenth century. Chiang Mai is situated about 300 metres (1,000 feet) above sea level. It is in the most mountainous part of the country, right in the middle of Thailand's great teak forests.

Thailand has a working population of about twenty-five million people. More than seventy per cent work in farming and fishing, and nearly eight per cent are employed in manufacturing trades. However, the country's most rapidly growing industry is tourism. This employs well over one million people, mostly in Bangkok and Pattaya, the country's leading seaside resort. Tourism is now growing very quickly and, after agricultural products, is Thailand's second largest source of foreign income.

Thailand has more than 100,000 different wild flowers. These include both herbaceous and perennial plants, and a wide variety of creepers. There are also countless different types of wild orchids, as well as ferns and bamboos.

Thailand also has two main types of forest. There is the evergreen forest, which accounts for thirty per cent of the forest

A view of the beach at Pattaya, Thailand's leading seaside resort. Water sports are a popular attraction

area, and consists of tropical evergreen, hill evergreen and mangrove. Then there is the deciduous forest. This accounts for the remaining seventy per cent of the forest area. Teak, one of Thailand's main exports, is a deciduous tree which grows in these vast forest areas.

There are 264 different species of mammals in Thailand. Most of the larger ones belong to the forests, and can now only be seen in the national parks. These include elephants, tigers (once abundant all over Thailand), rhinoceroses, hog deers, wild buffaloes, and various types of wild ox, including koupreys, gaurs and gayals.

There are also many smaller animals. These can still occasionally be found roaming wild in many parts of the country. They include bears, deers, tapirs, gibbons, squirrels, macaques, tree shrews, weasels, and scaly anteaters (pangolins).

Thailand is also rich in many different types of birds. In fact, no fewer than 860 different species have been recorded. Among the most common are pheasants, pigeons, minivets, hornbills, barbets, hawks, parrots, kingfishers, mynahs and various kinds of storks.

About ninety-five per cent of Thais are Buddhists. Buddhism was probably introduced into the country by King Mengrai in the thirteenth century A.D. It is the national religion of Thailand and the king is the "Defender of the Faith". One of the features of Thailand is its many Buddhist temples and shrines. These usually contain a statue of the Buddha sitting in a cross-legged position. Officially, dates in Thailand are calculated in relation

A fertile agricultural area in northern Thailand

to the year in which the Buddha was born (543 B.C.), just as we calculate our years in relation to the year in which Jesus Christ was born. But, in business nowadays, most people use the western calender.

The Thai language is spoken almost everywhere in the country, but there are many dialects, especially in the more rural areas. Several other languages are also widely used, such as Lao in the north-east, Malay in the south and Tiechew (a dialect of Chinese) in many different parts of the country. To western ears, Thai is a very strange-sounding language. Words can have up to five different meanings, depending on the pitch and tone used in speaking. The written language was invented towards the end of the thirteenth century and has forty-four consonants, plus dozens of vowels and tone marks.

Ancient Times

Some archaeological remains found in Thailand are more than five thousand years old. But they were not left behind by the people known as Thais. They are probably the relics of some Bronze Age community, who lived in the north of the country.

The first recorded inhabitants of Thailand, known as the Kmers, are thought to have settled in the north of the country in the eleventh century A.D. But soon afterwards the Thais began to move south from China. By the early thirteenth century a Thai, King Mengrai, and his followers had overrun almost the whole of the north. King Mengrai (the first Thai ruler known to us by name) is said to have founded the two cities of Chiang Mai and Chiang Rai. It is believed that he introduced the Buddhist religion into Thailand—a religion which was already quite widespread in India. King Mengrai also seems to have encouraged the Thais to move further and further south. By the time he died, at the age of eighty, the Thais were probably firmly established over almost all of present-day Thailand.

The next great ruler of Thailand was known as King Ramkamhaeng the Great, and his capital was a city called Sukhothai. He reigned from about 1280 to about 1317. King Ramkamhaeng introduced many new ideas to the country, both

This building, dating from the twelfth century, was built by the Kmers—the first recorded inhabitants of Thailand

in the arts and the sciences. He also invented the Thai alphabet, basing it on the one used in southern India.

After King Ramkamhaeng died, Sukothai began to decline. The Burmese were constantly invading it, and by the late fourteenth century the Thais had decided to abandon it. They established a new capital, much further away from the Burmese border, which they called Ayutthaya. It was only about 65 kilometres (40 miles) north of present-day Bangkok.

At about this time, the kings of Thailand began to regard themselves not just as kings but almost gods. Perhaps this was considered a useful means of maintaining power over the people in the more remote areas of the country. Although the king was

15

The ruins of Sukothai, the capital of King Ramkamhaeng the Great

considered divine, he was not allowed to be a tyrant. It was clearly understood that he only held his high office by the consent and will of the people. In fact, several kings of this period were overthrown because they were not thought to be acting for the benefit and happiness of their subjects.

By the seventeeth century Ayutthaya probably had a population of almost one million, and was larger than a great many of the European capitals at that time. It was a wealthy and charmingly exotic city, with palaces, temples and bridges —all built in a graceful and unusual style.

16

By then Thailand had regular contact with several European countries and a number of people from the West were even given places at court. However, this caused much unrest amongst the Thais, and from the end of the seventeenth century Europeans were almost completely banned from the country for one hundred and fifty years.

But there was one Western innovation which was clearly valuable—the new, up-to-date artillery weapons which were by then quite freely available in Europe. Up to this time, the Thai troops had usually been mounted on elephants and armed only with arrows or spears. But with these new weapons they believed that even on foot they would be much more successful in battle.

A huge statue
of the
Buddha in the
ruins of Sukothai

Over the years, the Thais had fought countless skirmishes and minor battles against their bitter enemies, the Burmese. But it was between 1763 and 1767 that the fiercest fighting took place and, despite all the Thais' modern weapons, the Burmese finally captured Ayutthaya. When the Thais later won it back they found the city merely a smouldering ruin. So their commander, Taksin, marched south and founded a new capital at a place called Thonburi. Taksin was then crowned king of Thailand. He reigned until 1782, when he was executed— because the people said he was mad.

After King Taksin's execution, General Phya Chakri came to power. He took the name of King Rama I, after a legendary Thai hero, and founded the Chakri dynasty which is still on the throne of Thailand today.

As the royal residence at Thonburi was too small, the King decided to build a larger palace on the other side of the Chao

A view of some of the *chedis*, or pagodas, in Ayutthaya. Ayutthaya was the capital of Thailand for about four hundred years, until the late eighteenth century

Part of the royal palace founded by King Rama I

Phraya River. This was in a tiny village called Bangkok— which thus became the fourth and greatest capital in the long history of Thailand.

King Rama I was followed by his son, King Rama II. Then came his son, King Rama III, who ruled from 1824 to 1851. During King Rama III's reign, Europeans were allowed back into the country and western influences began to spread there once more.

The next monarch, King Rama IV, was a well-respected ruler in Thailand. Unfortunately, most people outside Thailand know him only as a bad-tempered, short-sighted king portrayed in

19

the musical and film *The King and I*. But he was, in fact, a highly-educated man, who spoke seven languages and sent diplomats as far afield as England and France.

The ruler who followed, King Rama V, brought Thailand into the twentieth century. He abolished slavery, and set up schools, a museum, a national library and Thailand's first post office. His death in 1910 was a great loss to the country.

Later Times

After 1917, Thailand gradually became more involved in European affairs. King Rama VI had been educated at Cambridge, and when the First World War broke out he sent Thai troops to France to fight side by side with the British and Commonwealth forces. After the war, Thailand joined the League of Nations, a forerunner of the United Nations. (These organizations were both set up to try to keep world peace.)

By this time, many princes, courtiers and some sons of rich merchants were being educated in Europe. There they saw how a country could be ruled democratically, and some of them began to criticize their own country's system of government. Although capable ministers and officials were now being given powers by the king, many people thought the change was not taking place nearly quickly enough. As a result there was a bloodless revolution in Thailand in 1932. King Rama VII was forced to agree to a new constitution, limiting his powers and making the country a democracy. However, the king never really adjusted to this new idea, and he abdicated a few years later.

The next ruler of Thailand, King Rama VIII, was only a boy of ten when he came to the throne, and of course could not assume any real powers. In 1946, before he was able to take

The famous bridge over the River Kwai built by prisoners of the Japanese during the Second World War

over the reins of office, he was mysteriously shot dead in his bed at the age of twenty.

When the Second World War broke out, Thailand at once declared its neutrality. But, in December 1940, the Japanese asked permission to pass through Thailand to attack Malaya and Burma. The Thais refused, but the Japanese immediately attacked them and there was little the Thais could do but give in.

The Japanese then forced the Thais to declare war on the Allies. But the sympathy of most of the Thais was with Britain and the U.S.A. Later the Allies made a few bombing raids on

22

Thailand, but not a great many, as Thailand had little strategic significance.

Thailand's present ruler, King Bhumibol, Rama IX, came to the throne in 1946 on the death of his brother. But because he was only eighteen years old and still at university in Switzerland, King Bhumibol was not actually crowned until May, 1950.

This king has finally brought a measure of stability to Thailand. Although there have still been a number of revolts and uprisings, King Bhumibol is very popular with the Thai people. Many people regard him as being almost a god. A picture of the king, sometimes with other members of the royal family, hangs in almost every home, shop and factory. He is always greeted enthusiastically by throngs of people wherever he travels. When he was crowned he swore to "reign with righteousness for the benefit and happiness of all the people of Thailand", and he has obviously done his best to carry out this oath.

The king has always taken a active interest in new projects which will benefit his country. For example, he took the initiative in devising an artificial method of rain-making so that crops would grow in the more arid regions. He has also encouraged the digging of drainage canals to help areas damaged by flooding, and has started projects to reclaim swamp land for housing or farming.

The king never forgets that he is the Defender of the Buddhist Faith in Thailand. When he was a young man, King Bhumibol became a Buddhist monk for a time, as do nearly all young men in Thailand. In his speeches he frequently quotes from the Buddhist scriptures, and he makes it clear that he aims to rule the country in keeping with his religious beliefs.

King Bhumibol also has one rather unexpected accomplishment, however. He is internationally recognized as a very talented jazz musician and composer. The Thai people are very proud of this, although jazz is not particularly popular in Thailand. (The older people mostly prefer traditional Eastern music, and the younger people like the same pop music as Western teenagers.)

In 1950 King Bhumibol married the beautiful young Queen Sirikit. Like the king, Queen Sirikit is a direct descendant of King Rama V. As a child she spent a long time in Europe, including London where her father was the Thai ambassador, and she speaks English fluently.

The queen's royal duties involve visiting children as well as the sick and the old. She is particularly interested in people who live in the more remote areas of the country. In 1979 the United Nations presented the queen with a special medal only given to women ''who by their lives and their work have helped to uplift the status of women, particularly in rural areas'', in recognition of their efforts.

The queen has also set up a scheme to teach handicraft skills in rural farming communities. The queen's own staff often train young people who are then able to teach others. The type of work varies from place to place, but around Chiang Mai

Thailand is famous for the beautiful silk fabrics it produces. These girls are spinning the silk thread

embroidery and weaving have been very successful, as has silk production in the extreme north-east.

The king and queen have four children, three girls and a boy. The heir to the throne is Crown Prince Maha Vajiralongkorn, who was born in Bangkok in 1952.

1982 marked the two hundredth anniversary of the crowning of the first Chakri ruler, King Rama I. This was celebrated all over the country, but particularly in Bangkok—because King Rama I had decided to make his capital there.

Buddhism

No one can spend long in Thailand without seeing a Buddhist monk. They wear long, saffron-coloured robes covering all but their right shoulders. Most of them are aged between seventeen and twenty-two, though they vary from boys of ten to old men. All young men are expected to spend three or more months in a monastery. This is not compulsory, but people would think it rather odd if any young man did not want to do this. Because monks have to shave their heads, most young men decide to go into a monastery directly after their military service (which is compulsory by law) while they still have short hair!

There are also a few Buddhist nuns in Thailand. They wear white robes similar in design to the men's, and have their hair short but not shaved off altogether. Nearly all the nuns are widows who have decided, after the death of their husbands, to dedicate the rest of their lives to serving in the temples.

The founder of Buddhism, Gautama Siddartha, was born in India in about 500 B.C. He is said to have been a prince, and to have had a luxurious childhood. Later he spent many years meditating in the countryside, and when he returned to the city he began preaching a new way of living.

Before long he was called the Buddha, which means ''the enlightened one''. He did not lay down any definite rules or

creeds but put forward three very important ideas. The first was that violence of all kinds should be avoided, the second that people should not give way to their own selfish desires, and the third that death was not the end of a person's existence. In fact, Buddhism is based on a belief in reincarnation. It teaches people that they may live a great many lives and that if they commit sins in one life they may return as an animal instead of a human being in the next. The ultimate aim is to reach the state of perfect knowledge and happiness, called Nirvana, which is a kind of heaven. Everyone can achieve this, provided he or she has

27

followed all the Buddha's teachings as faithfully as possible in every way.

Buddhism originally became popular in India, as a reaction against the complicated Hindu religion. Many people did not like the strict class barriers and rituals of Hinduism, and found Buddhist thinking more tolerant and kind. Nowadays, however, Buddhism has almost died out in India, and Thailand is one of the few countries in the world where it is still the national religion.

At first light every morning, the Buddhist monks set off with their begging bowls to the nearest houses. They are never allowed to handle money, so the only way they can eat is to beg for food. Most people are pleased to give them something, as Buddhism teaches that they are conferring a favour on the householders by allowing them to give food to the monastery.

About midday the monks return to their monastery for their one meal of the day. After this they usually spend the rest of their time reading and meditating inside the monastery walls. They are not normally forced to stay entirely inside the monastery, and can go for walks or visit friends or relatives.

The monastery is usually built around the edge of the temple (*wat*) grounds. This is where the monks live, eat and sleep. There may also be a cloister-like area, sometimes with a number of small statues of the Buddha, where people can sit; and sometimes there are gardens with trees and grass, or even a small stream.

Inside the temple itself there is always a large statue of the Buddha. It usually shows him sitting cross-legged, and is nearly

28

A Thai housewife, giving food to a Buddhist monk

always brightly gilded. Sometimes the statue is also covered with tiny pieces of gold leaf which people buy to stick on it, either as a form of worship or possibly to pray for some particular favour.

Whatever the time of day there are nearly always people in the temples. They come to say a prayer or light a joss-stick, but they do not usually stay very long. When the monks meet together several times a day to chant and pray, the visitors do not join in the prayers but continue with their own private worship.

There is also a curious rattling sound in nearly all Buddhist

29

Worshippers in a Buddhist temple. Whatever the time of day, there are nearly always people in the temples—an indication of the importance of religion in everyday life for the Thais

temples. This is made by people shaking a long, cylindrical wooden box, filled with thirty or forty wooden spills. Once a spill has been shaken out the person takes it to an attendant who reads the number on the side of the spill, and then hands over a sheet of paper covered with writing. This paper is supposed to tell the person's future. It may say that a business transaction will turn out well, or that the person will meet a dark, handsome stranger! After reading it, the person takes two larger sticks with special markings on them and throws them up in the air. If they both land the same way up it is a sign that the prediction will come true, but if they land on different sides then the outcome is not so certain.

Visitors to some Buddhist temples have to take off their shoes. This is partly a sign of respect and partly to keep the dust from the streets out of the temple. Also, in all Buddhist temples it is strictly forbidden to sit on the ground with one's feet pointing towards the altar, as this shows disrespect to the Buddha—so feet must always be tucked under the body.

One sign of the strength of the Buddhist religion in Thailand is all the tiny shrines. These are found in the gardens of private houses and hotels, and even in garage forecourts and at the entrance to factories. A typical shrine looks rather like a doll's

Tiny shrines such as this can be seen all over Thailand—even outside factories and in petrol station forecourts

house on the top of a pole. Inside there is a small statue of the Buddha, with incense sticks, flowers or perhaps small offerings of food in front of it.

Buddhism is quite tolerant of other religious faiths. There is never any ill-feeling shown by Buddhists to the Hindu Indians who live in Thailand, or to the Malaysians who are Muslims. This is because Buddhism tries to show people how they should live, rather than teaching that certain beliefs are right and that all other beliefs are therefore wrong.

Bangkok

Bangkok was only a small fishing village until King Rama I decided to make it his capital in 1782. There was unlimited space to build a magnificent palace there, and the king thought he would be safer from his enemies, the Burmese, on the east side of the wide Chao Phraya River.

For tourists, one of Bangkok's main attractions is the Grand Palace. This is not just one palace, but a whole group of royal residences, temples, museums and offices. Sometimes described as a city within a city, its numerous buildings are crowded together inside a white wall nearly two kilometres (more than one mile) long.

The first four kings of the Chakri dynasty lived their entire lives within the walls of the palace. They were thought to be far too important to mix with ordinary people. Each king added new buildings, mainly in the traditional Thai style, with steeply sloping tiled roofs. However, there are also a few buildings in European style.

Three of the buildings in the Grand Palace are particularly fine. One is the magnificent Throne Hall, built in the reign of King Rama V. Here the king is crowned, whilst seated on the coronation chair under a nine-tiered white canopy. Then there is the Audience Hall of Amarindra, which also has a throne with a nine-tiered white canopy, as well as a golden boat-shaped altar. Finally there is the Audience Hall of Dusit Maha Prasad. This is a perfect example of a classical Thai palace, with its roof rising in four tiers and topped by a slim gilt spire.

There are also a number of temples, or *wats*, in the Grand

Wat Phra Keo, one of the temples in the Grand Palace. This temple contains the famous ''Emerald Buddha'', a small statue made of jasper

Palace. One of them, Wat Phra Keo, contains one of Thailand's most highly-prized religious images— the "Emerald Buddha". It is actually made of jasper and is only about 60 centimetres (2 feet) tall, but looks very imposing on top of its high golden altar. An interesting custom with this Buddha is that its clothes are changed with the seasons. In the hot season it wears thin robes, in the rainy season slightly thicker ones and in the cool season the thickest of all. Europeans may find this odd (especially because it is hot in Thailand even in the so-called cool season!) but it is a tradition that dates back to the very early days of the Chakri dynastly.

There are at least three hundred other *wats* in Bangkok. The oldest and largest is Wat Pho, which was founded in the sixteenth century when Bangkok was still only a village. Inside the temple is a huge statue of the Buddha, lying on its side. This statue is 46 metres (150 feet) long and 15 metres (50 feet) high.

Wat Arun stands on the far side of the river in Thonburi. It is covered all over with tiny pieces of shining pottery. The name Wat Arun means "Temple of the Dawn", and when the sun shines in the early morning it sparkles and looks quite magical.

Wat Saket stands on top of a high mound, and from the top there is a wonderful view all over Bangkok. But the Thai people do not climb it for the view. They go to visit the shrine, which is supposed to contain many small relics of the Buddha which were sent there from India.

Wat Trimitr is famous for its solid gold Buddha. This was

A view of Bangkok, taken from Wat Saket

only discovered in 1953 when a heavy clay Buddha was being moved by a crane. The statue was dropped and broke open to reveal the gold Buddha inside. Weighing five and a half tonnes, the Buddha is seven to eight hundred years old. It was probably covered with clay to prevent it being stolen by Burmese invaders.

Not far from the Grand Palace is the Pramane Ground. This is an immense open space, where a huge market with more than ten thousand stalls is held every Saturday and Sunday. Everything seems to be on sale there, from gleaming ceremonial swords to shirts and jeans, white mice dyed green and even a large variety of cats (including some Siamese ones!).

36

Unlike most modern cities, Bangkok has hardly any skyscrapers. Instead, there are long stretches of two-, three- and (less often) four-storey buildings. This means that Bangkok is a large, straggling city, with no real centre, although there are several areas which are extremely busy and important.

When Bangkok was first founded it had almost no roads. Instead, the whole city was criss-crossed by canals, or *klongs*, as they are called. The inhabitants of the city lived by the side of these *klongs*, and everything they needed was brought to them in wide, flat-bottomed barges. Then, in the 1860s, the "New Road" was built. Today this is still one of the main routes through the city and a major business area. A large number of European firms have offices there, as well as many important Thai firms. As time went on, most of the *klongs* were filled in and replaced by roads, and today Bangkok has some of the noisiest and busiest streets in the world.

Another well-known street in Bangkok is Ratchadamnoen Nok. It is a wide leafy avenue, with the Democracy Monument at one end. It is lined on both sides with government offices, many of them having the same steep roofs that are found on all traditional style Thai temples and palaces.

One reminder of Bangkok's past is the famous floating market. Every morning, the moment it becomes light, dozens of small boats (laden with everything from fish to vegetables) meet on a canal just outside the city. In recent years, however, the floating market has become much smaller. The only way to get some idea of what it was once like is to visit another floating market at Damnoen Saduak, about two hours' drive to the south-west.

Another relic of the past are the royal barges. When Bangkok had no roads the kings had to use these barges for all ceremonial occasions. Today thirty of these ornate, gilded boats are on show in the royal boat-yards. The largest and most graceful (which needs sixty oarsmen to row it) is still used for special state processions.

The Red Cross Snake Farm is one of the most unusual places in Bangkok. Dozens of gaily patterned cobras, spotted vipers

The solid gold Buddha in Wat Trimitr, discovered in 1953. This statue weighs five and a half tonnes and is over seven hundred years old

The royal barges—ornate gilded boats—on show in the royal boatyards. The largest is still used for some state processions

and banded kraits (a dangerous Indian snake) are kept here, along with numerous other poisonous snakes. Visitors can come and see the snakes being milked of their venom. This is then processed to provide anti-snakebite serum for use all over Southeast Asia.

Other Cities and Towns

Thailand's second largest city, Chiang Mai, is about 640 kilometres (400 miles) north of Bangkok. It stands on a plateau surrounded by some of Thailand's highest and most densely wooded mountains. It is a pleasant place, with far less noise and bustle than Bangkok and, being so high, there is almost perfect spring-like weather from October to January.

Originally Chiang Mai was surrounded by a huge city wall. It is said that King Mengrai the Great ordered it to be built in the thirteenth century. It took ninety thousand men, working shifts all round the clock, several months to complete it; and much of the wall can still be seen round the old part of the city today.

King Mengrai probably also founded the temple called Wat Chiang Mai. This contains the Crystal Buddha and the Marble Buddha. Another temple is Wat Doi Suthep, which stands on the side of a steep hill just outside the city, some 1,100 metres (3,400 feet) above sea level. Three hundred steps, with stone serpents on either side, lead up to it; but visitors are rewarded for the climb not only by the sight of hundreds of images of the Buddha but also by a superb view over the city.

Like European craftsmen in the Middle Ages, the craftsmen in Chiang Mai live in groups. For example, all the silversmiths

Making lacquerware bowls in Chiang Mai. Each craft is concentrated in one area of the city, where the craftsmen live and work

live in one district, hammering delicate patterns on bowls and trays all day long. There is also a district for the lacquerware workers, who use strands of coloured straw to decorate boxes and bowls, as well as areas where the wood-carvers and the furniture-makers live. Perhaps the most fascinating craft to watch is the umbrella-making. This is the traditional craft for village girls in Bor Sang, a little way east of Chiang Mai. A girl takes a length of bamboo and adds thin wooden spokes and a thin paper covering. Then she paints designs on the umbrella. Sometimes the customers even tell her what designs they would like!

The King of Thailand has his country home in Chiang Mai.

41

A young Thai girl, painting designs on paper umbrellas. This is a traditional craft practised by girls in the village of Bor Sang, near Chiang Mai

He and the rest of the royal family spend several months there every year to escape the heat and bustle of Bangkok. When the king is not in residence, the palace grounds are open to visitors. They can walk through the beautiful gardens and see the flowers which have been brought from many parts of the world.

A city with a similar name, Chiang Rai, is the capital of northern Thailand. Like Chiang Mai, it was founded in the thirteenth century by King Mengrai. According to legend, the king's elephant escaped and led him to a spot near the Mekong

42

River. The king decided to build a city there, partly because of the beauty of the site and partly because of its strategic position. Today Chiang Rai looks rather like a town in the Midwest of America, because the present-day town was laid out by an American missionary. It has some interesting old Buddhist temples, built on hill-tops just outside Chiang Rai itself, from which there are pleasant views of both the town and the river.

Lamphu, also in the north, is best known for its beautiful fabrics. It also has an ancient monastery, which is always crowded with people studying or meditating. The huge gold *chedi*, or pagoda, in the middle of the monastery was probably

The huge gold *chedi*, or pagoda, in the middle of Lamphun monastery. It is probably more than one thousand years old

begun more than a thousand years ago, before the Thai people themselves arrived in the country.

Only 160 kilometres (100 miles) north of Bangkok is Lop Buri which, in the seventeenth century, was considered second only to the capital, Ayutthaya. In Lop Buri there are the remains of a royal palace which must have been very imposing when it was first built. One feature of the palace is the many small niches in its high walls, in which lighted candles are placed during festivals. One of the many ancient shrines in the city is dedicated to a Hindu deity and houses a large troop of friendly monkeys. Visitors often buy a bunch of bananas to give the monkeys as they run around the shrine, but unfortunately the monkeys sometimes seem to think it is fun to steal the visitor's cameras or handbags!

Kanchanaburi is only a short distance from the famous bridge over the River Kwai. Near the bridge is a cemetery where more than eight thousand soldiers are buried. They were prisoners of war in Thailand under the Japanese, and died building the bridge and the railway. The bridge is constructed of huge iron girders. It is still used by trains two or three times a day, as well as by pedestrians and cyclists— who apparently know exactly when the next train is due.

South-east of Kanchanaburi is Nakhon Pathom, the oldest city in Thailand. It has the tallest temple in the country, some 100 metres (395 feet) high. This was begun in the mid-nineteenth century, and has a vast gold-tiled dome, inside which are the remains of a much older temple, built around A.D 150.

Phuket is the best-known city in the south of Thailand. It stands on Thailand's biggest island, linked to the rest of the country by a causeway. Many tourists visit Phuket because of its fine white sand and clear sea. (The Thais themselves cannot understand why foreigners enjoy sunbathing and swimming!) The sea all along the coast of Thailand is full of fascinating coral and brilliantly coloured fish, and underwater diving is a popular way for tourists to explore the variety of life below the sea-surface. People who are less energetic or not so good at swimming can hire a glass-bottomed boat and view things in a more leisurely way. Unfortunately, due to pollution, there is not as much to see as there used to be.

Another busy place in the extreme south is called Hat Yai. This town is only about 50 kilometres (30 miles) from the Malaysian border, and does a good trade in smuggling. It is also well-known for its bull-fights. In Thailand this does not mean a bull-fighter trying to kill a bull (as in Spain). Here, two specially-trained bulls fight each other until one becomes tired and ambles away.

The Klong People and the Hill Tribes

At one time *klongs*, or canals, were found almost everywhere in Thailand. But over the years many of them have been filled in and replaced by roads, especially those in Bangkok. However, there are still large numbers of people who make their homes beside the *klongs*, and who live their lives almost entirely around the water.

The homes of these *klong* dwellers are wooden houses built on piles. A typical house has just one floor, with an overhanging roof and a short wooden pier where a boat can be tied up. The *klong* dwellers spend nearly all their time out of doors. They use

A typical *klong*-dweller's home

The famous floating market at Damnoen Saduak — note the women's traditional lampshade-shaped hats

the *klong* for everything from washing themselves to washing their clothes.

Some of the *klong* dwellers cultivate a small piece of land behind their homes. Others work in the many timber yards found beside most of the *klongs* or run small shops or restaurants. *Klong* dwellers may also run garages, supplying petrol for the outboard motors of the long narrow boats, called *sampans*.

The *klongs* are at their liveliest first thing in the morning. From about half past five onwards, hundreds of *sampans*, all laden with produce, meet together at one or other of Thailand's famous floating markets. The best known of all is held in Thonburi

(Bangkok's industrial district), but by far the busiest and most exciting takes place at Damnoen Saduak, about 110 kilometres (60 miles) to the west.

Usually the woman in the family takes the goods to market. Dressed in traditional Thai clothes, with a hat like a wide straw lampshade, she not only steers the boat but also serves the customers. Most of the goods for sale are produced by the *klong* people themselves, and are mainly such things as water-melons, bananas and pineapples. Fish, meat and various household utensils are also on sale. There are always a number of floating cafés at the markets, selling tea, coffee and various canned drinks. It all makes a very colourful, exciting spectacle, and hundreds of visitors come every morning to watch, viewing it either from motor-boats or from one of the many small foot-bridges that cross the canals.

From time to time the canals have to be cleaned out. Then a householder will build two mud walls, one on either side of his house across the water. The thick, evil-smelling silt is lifted out of the canal by hand, put on carts and taken to the rice fields to be used as manure.

A much more primitive people are the hill-tribes who live north of Chiang Mai. They are a different race from the Thais, but no one is quite certain where they originally came from. They have a different language, religion and way of life from the people in the rest of the country; and over the centuries have had very little contact with the rest of the population.

Some of the best known hill-tribes are the Yao, the Meo and

the Akha. The Yao live only a little way north of Chiang Mai, while most of the other tribes live on the slopes of mountains at least 1,100 metres (3,500 feet) above sea level, where they believe they are safe from evil spirits.

Many of the hill-tribes live today in the same way as they have done for centuries. Their homes are rickety wooden houses on stilts, with a few pigs and dogs roaming around. The men plough the fields with the aid of water-buffaloes, while the women (with their babies strapped on their backs) mill the corn between two stones. In their traditional red and black costumes with beads or coins round their heads, these people look very

Meo children, members of one of the northern hill-tribes

Yao women in their traditional red and black costumes

attractive. However, the hill-tribesmen have had many problems over the years, partly because they are cut off from the rest of the world and are largely uneducated.

For example, the hill-tribes use a "slash and burn" method of agriculture. This means that people cut down and burn parts of the huge teak forests in order to grow their crops. In the short term this produces good harvests, but within five or six years the soil is exhausted and the hill-tribes have to cut down another area of trees. This is a very wasteful method of cultivation.

50

Gradually the forests are destroyed and it will take centuries to replace them. This reduces the amount of teak that can be produced, which is a serious loss to the Thai export trade. It also causes a change in the watershed patterns, which results in flooding in the plains and disrupts the rice cultivation there.

The cultivation of the opium poppy among the hill-tribes has recently reached enormous proportions in the "Golden Triangle" where Thailand, Burma and Laos meet. Opium has been illegally exported to Europe and America, where it fetches huge sums on the "black" market. This has been very worrying to the Thai government in recent years, and strong measures have been introduced to deal with the problem. The possession

An Akha village in northern Thailand—note the rickety wooden houses and poor living conditions

of heroin is punishable by terms of imprisonment varying from five years to life and by exceptionally heavy fines. The possession of marijuana is punishable by anything up to six months in prison.

Perhaps most worrying of all for the Thai government is the spread of terrorist gangs among the hill-tribes. These have mostly come across the border from neighbouring Communist countries, particularly Laos and Vietnam. They have used small hill-tribe villages as hide-outs, and several times in recent years

This land, once covered in valuable teak trees, has been cleared by burning so that the hill-tribes can grow their crops. The soil will soon be exhausted and the hill-tribes will have to cut down more trees

government troops have gone north to put down riots and revolts of various kinds.

The government has recently undertaken a massive education programme. Agricultural experts have travelled far, often on foot, to teach the hill-tribesmen about up-to-date farming methods. As a result, entire villages now grow peaches, beans, stawberries, coffee and a special kind of rice that will grow on hill-sides. This has largely put an end to the "slash and burn" farming methods. It has also slowed down the opium trade, which has never been as profitable to the Thais themselves as to the drug peddlers in the west. Volunteer teachers have set up mobile schools to teach the tribesmen to read and write, in the hope of bringing them into closer contact with the rest of the country.

Agriculture and Industry

Thailand's wealth lies in its land—in its agriculture, forestry, fisheries, mineral resources and, more recently, in its natural gas. Approximately forty-five per cent of the land is under cultivation, and a large proportion of the rest is either used for animal husbandry or is forested.

The main agricultural crop in Thailand in rice. Paddy fields cover vast areas of land, and are mostly ploughed by water-buffaloes. Rice is the staple food in Thailand. It is also one of the country's main exports and Thailand has recently become the world's second biggest rice exporter, after the U.S.A. Tapioca is also grown in the east and north-east of the country. Although much of it is used for home consumption, Thailand is also the world's largest tapioca exporter. Maize is grown extensively in most parts of the country, with two-thirds of the crop exported every year. Sugar-cane is grown in many different parts of Thailand, with most of the produce being sold in Thailand. Coffee has also been introduced into the country recently, but so far most of the bushes are rather immature, and the yield has not been very high.

In the south of Thailand the main crop is rubber. The liquid which comes from the rubber plant is called latex and half a million tonnes of it are produced annually. Nearly all the rubber

Harvesting rice, Thailand's main agricultural crop

is exported (two-thirds of it to Japan), making Thailand the world's third largest exporter after Malaysia and Indonesia.

Tobacco production has been increasing steadily in recent years and a Virginia-type tobacco is the kind that is most usually grown in Thailand. The Thai people themselves are not particularly heavy smokers, and two-thirds of the crop is exported every year.

Another very important crop is cotton. It is mostly exported in its raw state, but a certain amount is made into cloth for the home market. Jute, which is mainly used for mats or sacking, is also an important crop, and over 30,000 tonnes are exported every year.

Silk has been produced in Thailand for centuries. In fact, the Thais may have brought the art of silk production with them when they moved south from China. Thai silk can be made into anything from delicate blouses to heavy bedspreads and most of it is exported.

These women are taking the husks off coconuts—coconuts are one of the most important crops in the south of Thailand

A girl weaving silk in Chiang Mai. Thai silk is a valuable source of foreign income

One of Thailand's best known and most valuable products is teak. The trees mostly grow in the mountainous areas in the north, and the logs are deftly moved around by elephants. Nowadays nearly all the teak is made into furniture or ornaments of some kind, and then exported, mainly to Europe and America. In the great teak forests there is nearly always rattan, which is used for making cane furniture. Another commercial product from the forests is dammar, a resin which comes from the conifers and which is used in the maufacture of varnish and shellacs of various kinds.

Thailand ranks third in the world as a fishing nation. It has a fleet of over 26,000 fishing vessels, and an annual catch of about two million tonnes. The fishing boats mostly ply in the Gulf of Thailand and in the nearby South China Sea and Indian Ocean, and about half of the catch is exported.

Tin ore is by far the most important mineral deposit in Thailand. Most of the tin is found in the south of the country, near the Malaysian border. After Malaysia and Indonesia, Thailand is the world's third largest producer of tin, which is mostly exported to the United States, Japan and the Netherlands.

Thailand also has the world's largest deposits of potash. This is mostly used for fertilizers in Thailand itself, and very little

Working elephants near the city of Lamphun

Tin-mining at Phuket in the south. Tin-ore is the most important mineral deposit in Thailand

is exported. In addition, Thailand has deposits of gypsum, kaolin, copper, graphite, asbestos and rock salt.

People who like fluoride in their toothpaste probably never ask where it comes from. If they did, the answer might very well be Thailand. This non-metallic ore, which is also used extensively in steel production, is exported from Thailand in large quantities, particularly to Japan, the U.S.S.R. and the Netherlands.

Thailand has a large variety of precious and semi-precious stones. These include rubies, sapphires, emeralds and topaz.

There is also a certain amount of precious metal to be found in Thailand, and most of the stones are set in locally mined gold or silver and then sold as jewellery.

Thailand's latest discovery has been natural gas. It was first tapped in the Gulf of Thailand in 1981, but several other fields will soon be in operation as well. The first consumer of the gas was an electricity generating plant, but it is hoped that it may soon be available for all kinds of industrial purposes.

Education, Medicine and Transport

Until the late nineteenth century education in Thailand mainly took place in the *wats* (temples) and only boys were given any tuition. The pupils lived in the monasteries, and waited on the monks in return for their board and lessons. However, only a small number of parents sent their sons to be educated, and in any case the teaching was limited to the "three Rs" and religious and moral instruction.

The kings, however, were well aware of the value of education. King Rama III learnt to speak English so that he could read English books. He set up a number of schools. He also encouraged Christian missionaries to open schools and even employed European teachers for the royal princes.

King Rama IV continued the work begun by his father. He established a school in the palace so that the sons of court officials could be educated. Many boys from this school, and the king's own sons, later went on to schools and colleges in Europe.

Education gradually became more and more widespread in Thailand until, in 1892, a Ministry of Education was set up. In the same year the first Teacher's Training College was opened. It was called Chulalongkorn University, in honour of King Rama V who was sometimes known as King Chulalongkorn. In 1921 a law made schooling compulsory for

Buddhist monks studying in a monastery in Bangkok. Until the late nineteeenth century, this was virtually the only form of education available in Thailand

all children between the ages of seven and fourteen. However, this has never been completely possible because of shortages of both teachers and schools, especially in the more rural areas.

Today there are five educational grades in Thailand. The first is the kindergarten, for children aged 3½ to 7, which only a small number of children attend. Then comes the elementary school, which covers the years of compulsory education. Most children leave school after this.

For the children who stay on for the third grade there is a choice of three types of school. In each type of school, however, the course lasts for six years. There is a general course for those who are going to work afterwards, a training course for those going on to technical colleges and an academic course for those who wish to go on to university.

Unfortunately there are not nearly enough of these secondary schools, and many children are too poor to be able to take advantage of them. Although the teaching is free, the students have to provide all their own books and materials, and the government cannot help to pay for such things as meals or travelling expenses.

Some students go on to the fourth educational grade and spend two years at technical college. The first of these was opened in Bangkok in 1952. Today there are three similar colleges in the provinces as well, all preparing students to take jobs in engineering, agriculture or commerce.

Thai schoolchildren taking part in a physical education class

Pupils at a girls' secondary school in Bangkok. Unfortunately, Thailand still has too few secondary schools

For other students the fourth grade is a pre-university college. They have to spend two years there, which means that they are at least twenty-two before they can go to university. While they are at the pre-university college they have to study at least one foreign language. This is usually English, French or Chinese, because most text-books in Thailand are still written in one of these languages.

The last educational grade is a university. Thailand has eight universities, five of which are in Bangkok. It normally takes four years to obtain a degree (six for medicine or dentistry).

64

But a degree in agriculture or engineering takes only three years and a teacher's certificate only two.

After Chulalongkorn, the next oldest university in Thailand is Thammasat University. It is in Bangkok and was opened in 1934. Two more universities were founded in Bangkok in 1943, and the fifth, a university specialising in agricultural subjects, in 1948.

The first university founded outside Bangkok was Chiang Mai University. It was opened in 1965 in beautiful grounds on the edge of the city. This was followed by Khon Kaen University, and then by the Prince of Songkhla's University, which is the newest university in Thailand.

Education has now been compulsory in Thailand for well over sixty years, but still only about sixty per cent of Thais are able to read and write. However, this percentage is gradually improving as more and more schools are opened, particularly in the rural areas in the north.

There are also special problems in the south of the country. Most of the people there are Malaysians, and the children speak only Malay until they go to school. But, by law, at least fifty per cent of the teaching in schools must be in Thai—so the children then have to work in two languages, which is naturally rather a handicap.

In 1950 the United Nations started to help in Thailand's education programme. It has launched several training schemes in rural areas to teach young people a trade. The teaching is generally about agriculture and handicrafts, as these are the occupations most suited to these areas. A typical training centre is the one at Ubon, in the north-east. From here groups of teachers travel round all the neighbouring villages. They instruct young people in modern methods of agriculture and domestic science and where necessary also teach them to read and to write.

Medical care in Thailand is of a very high standard. There are well over four hundred well-equipped hospitals and clinics, staffed by highly trained doctors. Unfortunately, the medical care is not free, but the government is doing its best to ensure

Members of the Akha hill-tribe, including a young schoolgirl. Government-funded education programmes are bringing the hill-tribes into closer contact with their fellow-countrymen

that even the poorest people receive attention when they need it.

There are also approximately 6,500 health centres, where advice and treatment are given. Like the hospitals, they are not free, but there are usually special arrangements for the poor. These clinics are found almost everywhere in the country, although there are unfortunately still some isolated areas, such as the districts where the Hill Tribes live, where they do not exist.

Life expectancy in Thailand at the moment is much lower than in Europe or America. It is only 58 years for a man, and about 64 years for a woman. This is rapidly improving, however, now that such diseases as malaria have been largely eliminated (malaria is now found only in a few rural areas), and that the standard of nutrition is improving.

There is an excellent bus service in Bangkok and the other large towns in Thailand. The buses are extremely cheap, and there is a flat rate fare regardless of the length of the journey. A long-distance bus service links the various towns; and the buses on these routes are usually air-conditioned and very comfortable. There are countless taxis in Thailand, and these are also very cheap. Air-conditioned taxis are about double the price of the others, but even they are relatively inexpensive. In addition, there are large numbers of *samlors* for hire. In country areas, this means a small three-wheeled vehicle which the driver pedals like a bicycle; but in Bangkok a motorised three-wheeled vehicle is used.

The Thailand State Railway links Bangkok with all the other major towns in the country. It also connects with services in Malaysia, which run as far as Singapore. All the trains are pulled by diesel locomotives, and together they carry over 100 million passengers and well over 10 million tonnes of freight every year.

Thai Airways International operates from Bangkok's Don Muang Airport. Although it was only formed in 1959, it now carries more than two million passengers every year. Its fleet of planes, with their distinctive purple and gold livery, includes ten Airbus 300 planes and five Boeing 747s, as well as a number of other planes.

The domestic airline, Thai Airways, connects Bangkok with all the larger towns in the country. It also connects Bangkok

A busy street scene in Bangkok. This photograph shows a three-wheeled samlor, one of the most common means of transport

Passengers waiting for a train at Ayutthaya station. The Thailand State Railway connects all the major towns with Bangkok

with Kuala Lumpur and Penang (both in Malaysia), and with the capitals of Vietnam and Laos. The fleet consists at the moment of four Boeings 737s and six Avro HS 748s, and they carry an ever-increasing number of both tourists and businessmen.

Thirty-eight foreign airlines also use Don Muang Airport. For this reason the airport is now being enlarged and modernized. When the work is completed, more than 7,500 passengers will be able to use the airport every hour of the day.

Food and Drink

The main feature of Thai food is that it is extremely spicy. In fact it is so hot that most Europeans can only eat a rather watered-down version. The hottest ingredient is a tiny red or green chilli called *prik-kee-nooh,* which the Thais like to add to almost everything they prepare.

The Thais also eat a lot of steamed rice. This helps balance the spiciness of the peppers and gives bulk to the meal. The poorer people are, the more rice they tend to eat—because rice is by far the cheapest food available in Thailand.

A prosperous family may begin a meal with spring rolls— but a spicier kind than those sold in the West. The outside is a kind of delicate, crisp pancake, and inside there may be sweet and sour pork, crabmeat, bean sprouts or almost anything else the family like to eat.

Another starter, called *gai hor bai toey*, is served in a rolled-up leaf. Although it looks different from the spring roll the ingredients inside are often much the same. There may be chunks of chicken fried in sesame oil, soya sauce and oyster sauce, and extra flavour may be obtained by adding a few drops of whisky.

One of the most popular soups in Thailand is called *tom-yam-gung*. The broth is prepared with various herbs, and then pieces of chicken, fish or prawns are added. Once the ingredients are

Thai food is often very spicy. This lady is preparing a local delicacy

tender, lemon juice is added, along with *prik-kee-nooh*, and the soup is always brought to the table piping hot.

Fish is eaten by almost everyone in Thailand. Sometimes it is eaten raw, but it can also be cooked in a great variety of different ways. One popular dish is baked *pladook*, which is rather like a cat-fish. This is cooked with cloves, nutmeg and ginger, and served with chilli sauce. Crisp fried prawns are also popular with many Thai people. These are usually served with a choice of several different sauces. But most families will eat almost any type of fish, especially if it is fried and covered with one of their favourite sauces.

71

The Thais eat a lot of fruit. Fruit stalls such as this one can be seen throughout the country

For the main course a very popular dish is *gaeng pet*. This literally means "hot curry", and it can be made with pork, chicken, beef, fish or prawns. It has a slightly sweet taste because it is cooked in coconut milk, but it contains many different spices.

Gai yang is probably best described as barbecued chicken. It is one of the few Thai dishes which does not taste very different from a Western dish. A whole chicken is stuffed with grated coconut, and the chicken is then rotated on a spit over glowing charcoal. The coconut is removed before the chicken is served.

Desserts in Thailand usually look very attractive. However, they are often very sweet and sticky, and Westerners find them rather sickly. One of the most popular desserts is a sticky cold

72

rice, in which the grains are dyed pretty greens and pinks, and served with tiny chips of ice.

The Thais all eat a great deal of fruit. Oranges, bananas, melons and pineapples are all equally popular. The Thais also like *durians*, which are a kind of prickly plum. They smell just like rotten eggs, but are very sweet and juicy to eat. Mangoes are popular too, but they are only in season from March to May. Slices of mango are often served with rice cooked in coconut milk. Chilled mango, left to go nearly rotten, is also a popular dessert—especially powdered with grated ginger and poppy seeds.

Tea, coffee and soft drinks are all popular. Thailand also produces its own beer. Wine is not drunk a great deal because it is extremely expensive; but various spirits are quite popular, especially whisky.

Westerners are often surprised that there are no knives on the tables in Thailand. The reason for this is that the food is already cut up into small pieces before it is served. The table is normally laid with a fork on the left and a spoon on the right, although chopsticks are sometimes used with a stew.

In restaurants people are sometimes given a cold towel so that they can cool their hands and their faces. In fact, the towel is sometimes brought from the refrigerator. Similarly, better-off people nearly always have a cold face-towel beside their plates on the table at home, in much the same way as Westerners might have a serviette.

There are countless hawkers selling food in the streets in

73

Street hawkers, selling food in Bangkok — a well-established tradition in Thailand

Thailand. Most of them offer a large variety of nuts, as well as slices of water melon and pineapple. Some of them also sell meat balls and pastas stuck on skewers like kebabs so that they can be eaten in the street. Drinks of various kinds are also on sale. These include Coca-Cola and the more traditional Thai drinks, such as iced sugar-cane juice, lightly spiced and scented with cinnamon and cloves, and chilled lemon or lime tea.

Festivals

There can be few countries which have as many festivals as Thailand. They vary from small to large, and from lighthearted and amusing to solemn and religious. Most of them take place either in Bangkok or in Chiang Mai, although some are national festivals which take place nearly everywhere in the country.

A festival in January, marking the start of the western New Year, is a popular celebration. Many householders hang coloured fairy lights in their gardens, the temples are decorated and there are special Thai dances and games at the Pramane Ground in Bangkok.

In February every year comes the *Magha Puja*. This reminds people of the time when the Buddha gave a sermon containing all his teaching in front of 1,250 disciples. Buddhists go to their local temple to recite special prayers and then they make a clockwise procession round the temple carrying lighted candles.

The Flower Festival in Chiang Mai is also held in February. Both temperate and tropical flowers grow in abundance in Chiang Mai, especially in the early part of the year. A huge carnival is held, with long processions of flower-covered floats and parades travelling round the city.

April 6th every year is known as Chakri Day, because it was on this day in 1782 that General Phya Chakri was crowned as

75

Visitors to the Grand Palace in Bangkok, celebrating Chakri Day, the day on which General Phya Chakri was crowned as King Rama I. They are visiting the royal temples to show their love and respect for the monarchy

King Rama I. The main celebrations take place in the grounds of the Grand Palace in Bangkok, where thousands of people visit the royal temples, to show their love and respect for the monarchy.

April 13th is *Songkran*, the Thai New Year. This is a boisterous, fun-filled time. In Bangkok the festival begins with a long procession of floats, representing all kinds of groups and organizations. There are many bands playing a variety of curious eastern instruments. Then there is a huge fair on the Pramane Ground. Groups of Buddhist monks sit under a huge awning waiting for people to place gifts at their feet. There are also countless bird-sellers, as setting free a caged bird is thought to bring good luck. Another traditional activity is to sprinkle

76

water on the Buddha images, on the monks and on any older, respected people. In recent years, however, this has tended to become mainly an amusement for children and teenagers. Instead of water they usually use a kind of thin whitewash, and they all try to see how many of their friends or even casual passers-by they can splash with thin streaks of white.

The *Songkran* festival is particularly lively and colourful in Chiang Mai. This is probably because the people there are not as sophisticated or restrained as many of the modern Bangkok city-dwellers. Besides processions and fairs, there is dancing in the streets, often lasting for hours, and there are beauty contests for the girls, which always attract large crowds.

In May there is the Royal Ploughing Ceremony in Bangkok. This is held on a date fixed every year by the king's astrologers, to open the rice-planting season. There are several kinds of traditional ceremonies and processions on the Pramane Ground at which the king and queen are present. The whole festival is designed to ensure a good rice harvest.

Also in May is *Visakha Puja*. This commemorates the Buddha's birth, and conversion and his passing into *Nirvana*. Many temples all over the country are illuminated with thousands of paper lanterns, and there are torchlight processions and sometimes firework displays.

Then there is the *Boon Bong Fai*, or Rocket Festival. This is also held in May, mainly in the smaller towns and villages in the north-east of Thailand. The aim is to ensure a good rainy season, so that the crops will grow. However, the festival is

chiefly known for its drum-playing and its exciting displays of homemade fireworks.

October 23rd is King Chulalongkorn Day. This is held every year in remembrance of King Rama V, who was also called King Chulalongkorn. Thousands of people pour into Bangkok to lay wreaths of flowers at the foot of the king's statue, to show their gratitude for all that the king did for the country.

The rainy season usually ends towards the end of October. To celebrate this one of the most magnificent spectacles of the year often takes place in Bangkok. The king goes in his royal barge, accompanied by several golden barges, to Wat Arun, and gives the monks new yellow robes and various other gifts, as a thank-offering.

Perhaps the most beautiful of all is the *Loi Krathong* Festival. This is held on the night of the full moon in the twelfth lunar month (usually early November). It has no connection with any Buddhist rites or beliefs, and is probably a survival of ancient

78

The tug-of-war at the Elephant Round-up in Surin

spirit worship, when offerings were made to the water gods. People make little boats out of banana leaves, and put a candle and one or two incense sticks inside them. Alternatively, they may buy little boats, which are often in the shape of a swan or duck. Then they go to the nearest river and sing their favourite folk songs as they place the fragile craft on the water and watch them float away down the stream.

In November comes the Elephant Round-up at Surin, in north-eastern Thailand. Two hundred or more elephants are rounded up, and demonstrations are given of how they are caught and trained. Then comes the highlight of the event, which is a tug-of-war between a hundred men and one elephant. Occasionally it is a fairly even match, but usually the elephant wins hands down!

Games and Sports

Thai people are great sports enthusiasts. Nearly all Western games are popular, from football to golf. The Thais also enjoy numerous traditional Thai sports, some of which are only played in particular parts of the country.

The best known Thai sport is probably Thai boxing or *Muay Thai*. Every match begins with ritual prayers, followed by homage to the king. Then a small band (usually consisting of a pipe, some drums and cymbals) strikes up and the fighting begins, to the accompaniment of the music.

Unlike Western boxers, Thai boxers do not just use their fists. Blows with the feet, elbows and knees are all normal parts of the game. The main skill is in knowing which parts of the body to use for striking the blows. Throwing an opponent, however, usually only results in loss of points.

Thai fencing, *Krabi Krabong*, is probably as old as the Thai nation. A great variety of weapons can be used, such as quarter-staffs, sticks and wooden spears. But the most usual method of fencing is for each of the fighters to have two wooden sabres, and to hold one in each hand. Like boxing, Thai fencing is always accompanied by music. This begins very slowly, while the fencers make slow, ritual strokes. As the fight becomes more serious, the music is played faster and faster. It reaches an

80

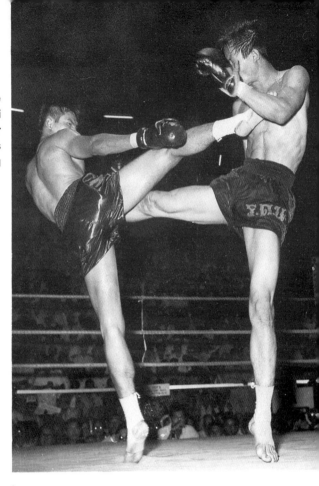

Thai boxing. Unlike Western boxers, Thai boxers may use their feet, elbows and knees in fighting

exciting climax when one of the fighters defeats his opponent.

Wicker-ball or *trakraw* is popular all over the Far East. In fact, it forms part of the Asian Games (the Eastern version of the Olympic Games). It is not only played by highly-trained professionals, but is also very popular among ordinary young men, who want to enjoy themselves after work or at the weekends.

There are various forms of *trakraw*, such as net *trakraw* and

81

The ancient sport of Thai fencing. A variety of weapons may be used and — like Thai boxing — Thai fencing is always accompanied by music

circle *trakraw*. But the most popular in Thailand is almost certainly loop trakraw or *Trakraw Huang*. A team of seven players stand round a 16-metre (50-feet) diameter circle, and they try to hit a ball through any one of the small hoops which hang 6 metres (20 feet) above the ground, without using their hands. However, unlike netball or basketball, the number of points gained varies according to the style and difficulty of the shot. Simply kicking the ball scores lowest, while the highest point-scorer is a shot in which the player flings both feet up in a back kick and sends the ball flying up into the ring.

Sabah is a game like skittles that is only played during the

82

Songkran festival. Instead of a ball, the flat, hard seed of a huge forest creeper is used. The popularity of the game originally arose from the fact that it was played by both boys and girls. This was considered very daring in the days when girls were normally carefully chaperoned.

The most colourful Thai sport, however, is the traditional kite-fighting, *Kaeung-Wau*. This takes place on the Pramane Ground in Bangkok between February and April, when the south-east wind is blowing. Thousands of people come to watch, spreading out their mats on the ground, while hawkers go round trying to sell them cold drinks and prawns.

According to tradition, all Thai kites are either male or female. (This has nothing to do with the bright pictures painted on them, which may be anything from an owl to a cat.) *Chula*, the male kite, can be as long as 2 metres (6½ feet) and is shaped like a five-pointed star. *Pakpao*, the female kite, is only about 75 centimetres (2½ feet) long, and roughly the same shape as a conventional kite.

The basic aim of Thai kite-flying is to try to drag down the opposing kites. At least two *Chula* kites have to be flown from one side of a line and four *Pakpao* kites from the other. The two team captains have to tell the men who actually fly the kites how to manoeuvre them and the men flying the kites are helped by a number of small boys who run with the string. The *Chulas* have bamboo barbs attached to the string near the kites. These are designed to entangle and force down the *Pakpao* kites. But the dainty *Pakpaos* are very speedy and difficult to catch. They have a semi-circular loop with which they can ensnare and drag down the large *Chula* kites.

The *Chulas* are usually, but not always, the winners. If two *Pakpaos* work together they can sometimes snatch an unexpected victory. Whatever the result kite-fighting always produces enormous excitement, partly because many of the people watching have placed a bet on one of the teams.

There are also several traditional sports involving animals. One of them is cock-fighting, which is banned in Bangkok but still very popular in the south. It is like cock-fighting in Europe in the Middle Ages, and again everyone likes to bet on the result.

Bull-fighting, *Chon Wua*, is also popular in the south. Two specially trained bulls lock horns, and each one struggles to make

Bull-fighting, Thai style. In Thailand, bull-fighting does not mean a bull-fighter trying to kill a bull (as it does in Spain). Here, two specially-trained bulls struggle against each other until one of them gives way

the other give ground. Bull-fighting fans will happily spend over eight hours watching fight after fight, and betting on the results. To Western eyes, however, it is a very slow, dull sport.

Fish-fighting, *Gad Pla*, is officially banned in most cities, but it still takes place. Two male Siamese fighting fish are put together in a jar, and a life or death battle begins. They are very attractive, large blue and orange freshwater fish. In certain parts of the country they are kept purely as pets, although two males cannot be kept together or they will fight.

Entertainment

The artistic life of Thailand came from a mixture of ancient Chinese and Indian influences. In recent years, however, most Thais have been turning more and more to Western forms of entertainment, so the traditional arts are often just tourist attractions nowadays.

Classical Thai dancing is an art that has largely died out. But it can still be seen in some places, such as the Lakmuang shrine at Bangkok. Here people pay dancers (who are always on call) to perform traditional steps. This is a way of giving thanks to the spirits for special favours.

The dancing at the Lakmuang shrine is known as *Lakhon* dancing. It is generally peformed by an all-female company, wearing glittering costumes and tall pointed head-dresses. The story is usually based on a Hindu epic called the *Ramayana*. There is sometimes a little speaking, but usually most of the story is conveyed by movement and gesture.

Another type of classical dancing is the *Khon*, or masked, dance. This is performed by both men and women, and the principal dancers always wear masks representing either demons or monkeys. *Khon* dancing is also based on the *Ramayana*, but it is extremely vigorous and strenuous, and the dancers need years of training before they are ready to perform.

This picture shows *Lakhon* dancers wearing glittering costumes and tall pointed head-dresses. They act out a story through their movements and gestures

The famous finger-nail dance originated in the north of Thailand. The dancers (who are all women) wear beautiful golden-coloured artificial finger-nails, sometimes almost as long as their fingers. Then they make certain stylized movements with their hands as they dance, which not only produce fascinating patterns but also convey traditional ideas.

The traditional music of Thailand has always been played mainly to accompany dancing. Particular types of melodies help to express various moods and actions. For instance, there are seven tunes to show when someone is thinking, thirteen to show anger, and no less than twenty-one to show sorrow or regret. These tunes are played on at least fifty traditional musical intruments. The instruments are all of Indian origin, although only specific instruments are used with any particular dance. For example, the *Khon* dancing is always accompanied by a *piphat* orchestra, which consists of one woodwind instrument, some xylophones and a variety of gongs and drums.

The famous Thai shadow play is called *Nang Talung*, meaning "puppets of animal skin". Life-size puppets made of ox-leather are used, and candles cast their shadows on a screen. Nowadays these shadow plays have almost died out. However, leather puppets of all sizes are still on sale, and are very popular with tourists who like to frame them and hang them on their walls.

Nearly all of Thailand's ancient books were lost when Ayutthaya was sacked in 1767. However, some romantic poetry written in the seventeenth and eighteenth centuries still exists as well as a little eighteenth century writing. In recent times members of the royal family have been some of the best known Thai writers. King Rama V (1868 to 1910) was thought to be one of the best authors of his day. His son, Rama VI was also a writer and made some very good translations of Shakespeare.

The first modern novel, *Yellow Race—White Race,* was written by a Thai prince, about his experience as a westernized young Thai man. Since then countless novels, and short stories and biographies have appeared in Thai bookshops, together with many translations of modern Western books.

All the Thai newspapers are published in Bangkok. There

Traditional Thai shadow plays have now almost died out, but puppets such as these can still be bought and are popular souvenirs for tourists

are fifteen daily papers in the Thai language, eight in Chinese and even two in English. They are generally written to entertain people rather than to give them information and only about a quarter of a million copies are sold each day.

The Thai radio stations are all government controlled. Most of the broadcasts are naturally in Thai, but there are also daily transmissions for several hours in Malay and Chinese. The radio is very popular in Thailand (particularly musical and educational programmes), and every village has at least one set which everyone tries to crowd round.

Television began in Thailand in 1955. The television sets, which are still mainly black and white, are quite expensive, but no licence is needed. Most of the programmes shown are made in Thailand, but foreign programmes are also shown, including American cartoons, which are extremely popular with the Thai children.

The Land of Smiles

Here is a list of dos and don'ts for visitors to Thailand. Most of them probably seem trivial, but they are all extremely important to the Thais.

First and foremost, the monarchy is greatly revered. So the slightest disrespect, even to a coin bearing the king's head, could have serious consequences.

Similarly, religion plays a very important part in Thai life. This means that visitors must be careful not to offend against any religious custom or practice. For example, visitors must never go into a temple wearing shorts or low-cut dresses, but must dress discreetly and modestly, however hot and sticky the weather. Also visitors must take off their shoes before entering the inner part of the temple. And women must remember not to speak directly to a monk or a novice, and certainly must not touch him. In fact, if a woman wants to give anything to a monk she must ask a man to tell him to spread out part of his saffron robe and then she can place her gift on that.

To Thais the head is the most important part of the body. So no one must ever touch another person, even a child, on the head. Thai people themselves always try to keep their heads lower than the head of any person who is older or more important than they are, to show their respect for him. In the same way there are rules concerning the feet. These are considered lowly, and must never be used, for example, for holding back a door. Moreover, no one must ever sit with their feet pointing towards a statue in a temple, or at some other person, but must always tuck them underneath their body.

When Thais meet each other, they do not shake hands or embrace as people in the West would. Demonstrations of affection are not allowed in public in Thailand. Only very Westernized young Thais would even dare to hold hands in the street, and touching other people at all is unusual. The most usual form of greeting is the *wai* greeting. In this, each person puts their hands together—as if saying a prayer—and bows to the other person. In recent years, however, some Thais have begun shaking hands with foreigners, instead of giving the traditional *wai* greeting, to make the visitors feel at home.

How much longer will these rules last? Nobody knows. Most of them are very old and it seems as if they will go on for ever. But the number of tourists in Thailand has doubled in less than ten years, and while the tourists are learning about Thailand, the Thais are also learning about the ways of the rest of the world.

Index

94